I, MARY

LINDA KAY

authorHOUSE®

AuthorHouse™
1663 Liberty Drive
Bloomington, IN 47403
www.authorhouse.com
Phone: 1 (800) 839-8640

Edited by Jane Goltz

Published by AuthorHouse 01/29/2019

ISBN: 978-1-5462-7831-3 (sc)
ISBN: 978-1-5462-7830-6 (e)

Print information available on the last page.

This book is printed on acid-free paper.

Scripture quotations marked TLB are taken from The Living Bible copyright © 1971. Used by permission of Tyndale House Publishers, Inc., Carol Stream, Illinois 60188. All rights reserved.

Contents

Part 1 Youth

Introduction... ix

Chapter 1   My Nazareth.. 1

Chapter 2   Becoming a Woman 7

Chapter 3   The Betrothal 14

Chapter 4   The Signs..21

Chapter 5   Elizabeth's story. 27

Chapter 6   Joseph 32

Chapter 7   Fear in Reality 37

Chapter 8   To Bethlehem 42

Chapter 9   Through Jerusalem to Bethlehem 47

Chapter 10   The Nativity.. 52

Part 2 Wife and Mother

Chapter 11   59

Chapter 12   Egypt...65

Chapter 13   Alexandria 73

Chapter 14   Jesus at Temple 78

Part 3 Jesus

Chapter 15   Jesus Begins His Ministry.......................... 85

Chapter 16   Jesus in Jerusalem 89

Chapter 17   New Life.. 94

Acknowledgements.. 99

References 101

About the Author..105

PART I

YOUTH

INTRODUCTION

My name is Mary of Nazareth. My story begins when I am little more than a child, just thirteen years old. My family and my God are my life. Each day I work at the tasks before me, always in prayer. My mother and father share the scriptures with me in stories, some spoken and some in song. The hope for my future lies in having a family and bearing children. The Jewish town of Nazareth sits in a valley, surrounded by green hills and stately mountains. We raise goats, chickens, and a few cattle. Vineyards provide a source of income and sustenance for my people, as well as the orchards and the fields of vegetables. We worship in a small synagogue, where the boys in the town go to school to learn the Torah. Girls learn from our families in the Jewish tradition, and all of us dream that someday one of us might be the chosen mother of the Messiah, the king who will come to save all of Israel.

CHAPTER 1

MY NAZARETH

Wind whistled through the cypress trees as I made my way through the courtyard to the community well. Dust from the surface of the hard earth invaded my sandals and worked between the toes of my feet as I walked. I kept my eyes on my feet on the familiar path, offering a prayer in praise of the oncoming spring and the sunshine that greeted my day. I balanced the clay jug of water on my shoulder, its weight softened by the folds of my dress and tunic.

The animals in their pens were making their early morning pleas for food. The goats bleated and the chickens crowed and clucked. A small calf nursed at his mother, butting her bag to make the milk flow. Women dropped in hay and sprinkled straw in the pens for bedding. I gathered my tunic closer to keep out the chill of the wind.

"Mariamme!" I heard my friend call me by my Hebrew name. I glanced behind to see Rachel approaching and set down my vessel. "Wait for me, so that we may draw water together." She caught up to me, just a little breathless from her pursuit, her long hair blowing in the breeze. Rachel, like me, wore a dress for working, a weave of scratchy wool tied with a leather belt. Our tunics were long, the color of the sheep, and brushed the ground.

I returned the clay jar to my shoulder and continued walking beside Rachel. "Is your family well?" I asked.

"My grandmother is ill, and we have been caring for her. We think she will be okay, but always fearful of her age. She is very fragile. You must come to my home for the celebration of my betrothal to Reuben. I am so nervous just thinking about it."

"I am happy for you, Rachel. Have you made your new clothes for the celebration? What color have you dyed the wool?"

"We have chosen a rose color, made from the pomegranates. My mother is helping me with the beading and design on the belt. Reuben comes from a good family. I pray that God will watch over me in the marriage and bless us with many children. He is working with his father in the vineyards, getting ready for the new crop. The vines must be trimmed and ready for the new fruit."

I set down my jug, turned to touch her cheeks and felt their warm softness. "You will be beautiful, and I am very happy for you." We arrived at the well and waited for our turns to draw water. Many women now gathered at the well, sharing events and telling stories. The hum of their conversations reminded me of the bees buzzing in their hives. They shared stories of their children, of their daily duties, and of the ancient history of families.

"I have heard that you will be betrothed soon as well, to Joseph." Rachel spoke above the din, as we reached the well.

I lowered my water jug into the well with the ropes. When I brought it up, I first filled Rachel's, then lowered it again to draw for myself. The ropes burned my hands as the heavy jug descended.

"Thank you, Mary. You are always so thoughtful. But you didn't answer my question."

Retrieving the jug, I poured a small amount of water into a bowl beside the well for a dog, who lapped at the water voraciously. "It is true. My father will announce the date, but not until the time comes. We have all grown up together in this town. Our families have been talking about Joseph to be my husband. He is a builder and a carpenter and works in the city with his father. He is a good man."

"You must be working on your new clothes for the celebration. Come and walk with me back home, so we can talk along the way. What is news from your house, Mary?" We walked across the courtyard and approached the high, blank walls of the buildings surrounding the area.

"We are more crowded, as my aunt has given birth to yet another baby. He is so beautiful. They will be taking him to

Temple soon for naming. Joseph has a smaller family, so if we marry we should have more room. What about Reuben? You will be moving to his home next year, right?"

"Reuben has a small family. That might mean more work for me, though. I have had some experience in the vineyards. At my home, I am learning to prepare fine meals for my family. There is so much work for us. My hands are already calloused." Rachel held out her hand to show me, rolling her big brown eyes.

"The work keeps us busy. I will be outside this afternoon tending the animals and continuing my needlework, if you would like to join me there. Now I have chores to do. Thank you for keeping me company." I turned toward my home, smiling at my friend's concern for the work of a new bride. Rachel was a girl of high spirit. I continued down a narrow path between the houses, balancing the water jug on my shoulder as I turned sideways to pass a small donkey in the walkway.

Reaching the door to my home, I heard the baby crying inside. My aunt looked tired and perplexed. "Please let me take care of the baby for you while you rest," I said, as I set the water down and reached for the baby. "I can take him for a little walk outside, and maybe he will go to sleep."

"Bless you, Mary. There is so much to do here in the house, and the baby is unsettled. I will take your advice and rest for a short while." My aunt laid back on her mat. I unwrapped the swaddling clothes on the baby and washed him with water and salt. I replaced the tight cloths first, then wrapped him in a shawl and held him close to me. A song from the Psalms offered a prayer for his peace. I looked forward to the day when my own baby would fulfill my life. I left the house to retrace my steps back to the courtyard, the open air and sunshine. The baby soon stopped his crying and fell asleep in my arms. I crept quietly back to the house and laid him down beside his mother, now fast asleep.

My mother beckoned to me, as she worked at the loom to weave new woolen fabric from the yarn cards. "You could shell those nuts for us, while I tell you a story." Jewish women shared stories from long oral history with the girls in the family, as only the boys learned to read the Torah. Stories told from memory were entertaining. Mother spoke in Aramaic, first offering a prayer. As she spoke, I listened carefully, shelling the nuts with my calloused hands, now discolored from the shells. The story began with Noah building the ark. I always so enjoyed imagining the animals arriving in pairs to board the ark for the long journey. My mind could not comprehend where they would all fit or how they would be cared for, but in my heart I knew the story was true. After all, my mother told me.

Later that day, following a light lunch of bread and honey, I met Rachel in the courtyard. We both helped to care for the animals in the pens, cleaning up the soiled straw and replacing it with clean scatters. They enjoyed the fresh, cool water we drew from the well. At Rachel's home, we climbed the ladder to the roof, where we could enjoy the sunshine as we worked. A short wall made sides around the roof, and we tucked ourselves into one corner, chattering excitedly about Rachel's upcoming betrothal ceremony. We giggled at the thought of being with a man.

Chapter 2

BECOMING A WOMAN

Early the next morning, the common area in the town was alive with merchants selling their wares.

"Come over here young lady, to purchase the finest sandals for your pretty feet! And at a bargain price."

I rushed past the merchant with my head down to avoid any eye contact with the man as is our custom, and wove my way between the displays as I walked to the well for our daily water supply. Men shouted, dogs barked, and women walked from place to place inspecting the goods. Filling the jar quickly, I hurried back to the house to tell my family of the merchants and the chaos. With shekels in hand and trade items in baskets, the women bustled through the alleys to the courtyard. I followed closely behind Mother, noticing an unfamiliar cramp in my abdomen.

I watched with admiration as Mother bartered with a mat maker for new mats. Her dark brown eyes sparkled in her fierce negotiations.

"At your price, I could buy ten mats in the city!" She started to walk away.

The merchant looked after her with a weary smile. "Okay, I'll bring the price down just to please you. Fifteen shekels, and that is the bottom price."

She also had her eye on a basket large enough to carry laundry to the creek. "This basket would serve me well, but the weave is shoddy. It will fall apart in a month! Do you have any baskets with a better weave?"

"Ma'am, this was done by my best weaver. He takes the utmost care in his weaving. This is the only one I have with me today. What can I do to send this basket home with you?"

After what seemed like a long argument with the merchant about the quality, she traded some fresh honey and olives for the basket. In the sack she brought with her, she gathered fresh pomegranates and melons from another merchant. She and other women chatted among themselves, greeting and sharing plans for dinner that evening in the courtyard. Each family would prepare for their own, but would share among friends.

"Mama, look. There is a poor man beside the well. Can we spare him some food?" He appeared to be blind, and his clothes were worn and dirty. There were no sandals on his feet. A sturdy stick to aid his walk lay beside him.

My mother handed me a pomegranate and some nuts. "Take this, and God bless you for your kind heart, Mary."

The man took the gifts and held my hand tightly. "Bless you, child," he said. "God is with you."

As we returned to the house, I noticed a bright red spot on my foot. "Mama, I am bleeding."

Since I had observed the practices of other women in the house, I knew this meant that my menses cycle had begun. Mother helped me secure a cloth and fasteners from the designated box, and happily shared the exciting news with others. This was cause for celebration. I had become a woman, now eligible to be betrothed. Plans began to take shape to share the good news. *Betulah* means 'young woman of marriageable age' in Aramaic or a*lmah* in Hebrew. The dinner planned for the evening quickly changed from a mere social meal to plans for a party to share with the small community of Nazareth.

Father slayed and butchered a goat, and set it to cooking on a spit above a fire in the courtyard. The muscles in his arms rippled with his skillful work, cutting through the hide and removing the entrails. Edible parts of these, the heart and liver, were a delicacy of the feast. The aroma of the cooking meat increased the anticipation for the joyful occasion. My aunt pierced my ears and inserted a pair of gold earrings passed down through the family, in preparation for the celebration. My earlobes throbbed in pain. Cleaned fish dried in the warm sun. Vegetables for the feast included beans, lentils, cucumbers, leeks, and onions. Pomegranates and melons would serve as dessert.

I found myself excited but embarrassed by the attention and the fact that everyone now knew of my womanhood. That feeling passed as my friend Rachel joined me to watch the men perform the story of David and Bathsheba. One man pretended to be Bathsheba, hiding his face behind a small fan, while another was King David. The crowd reacted to all the antics while the men depicted a sinful David as he viewed Bathsheba bathing.

"Mary, can you imagine? I will never be able to bathe in the pool again! You will have to go with me. And having adulterous relations with King David?" Rachel and I were horrified at the thought of a man watching us as we bathed. King David was such a sinful man, yet faithful to and favored by God.

We returned home late in the evening. "Mary, you do not have to fetch the water in the morning, as you can enjoy an easier schedule of work during your cycle," Mother informed me.

The next morning, my thoughts returned to the courtyard and the beggar, and I remembered another family in need.

"Mama, do you have some herbs and remedies we could share with the family of James? I could go through the courtyard with a basket and gather remaining morsels of food left from the celebration." James had been ill for some time, and with no work for income, they were suffering.

"I'll prepare some for you, Mary. And please relay our concerns and prayers."

Ruth, the wife of James, welcomed me and thanked me for bringing the gifts. I offered a prayer with Ruth for her husband's good health, including thoughts from Mother.

The menses for this first time lasted only a few days. After the cycle, I was required to bathe from head to toe in a special pool of clean water called a *mikvah*. This pool, set at the edge of town for privacy, was deep enough for complete immersion. A large, circular tank beside it gathered clean rainwater, spilling over into a smaller pool at the entrance for washing hair, hands, and feet before immersion into the main pool. I hesitated before entering the water, looking to see if my reflection looked any different after this ceremonious event. *I still look the same: same brown eyes, same long dark hair.*

After my bath, I donned clean clothes, constantly looking for any person who might be watching me, like King David. The antics of the actors were still in my mind. Feeling refreshed and ready to return to my chores, my day began by grinding barley for bread and making cheese curds from fresh goats' milk. The bread and curds served as a good breakfast. I checked on the fermenting wine in the barrels. Using the new basket my mother purchased at the market, I toted the family clothes to the river to wash them with lye soap and lay them out to dry on rocks. On my way back, I gathered a few eggs and caught two unsuspecting chickens to kill and process for the evening meal. *Someday I will do this for my own husband and family.*

The relatives gathered with Joseph's family in the evening to discuss my impending betrothal. I sat quietly and listened to their discussion, my heart pounding in my chest. *Can this really be happening?*

"Joseph offers comfort and security for Mary as he is gainfully working as a carpenter and builder, a trade learned from you, Heli. He is just a few years older, but already responsible as a man, and your family is very similar to ours." Father presented his endorsement to the rest of the adults gathered around him. Members of my family knew Joseph's ancestry and lineage as well as my own.

"Joseph is a student of the Scriptures, is devout in his knowledge of the Torah, and attends classes at the synagogue here in town, Jachim," added Joseph's father. Since there were only about 350 to 400 people in Nazareth, my family expressed how fortunate I was to have such a fine selection in Joseph. There were nods of approval around the room.

"We have observed Mary's devotion and kindness on many occasions, and Joseph has indicated his preference as well," Heli added. I am sure I blushed at his kind comment.

The betrothal ceremony was set to take place the next month, and the contract drawn between the men of the families. The next day Joseph brought me a donkey as a token of his betrothal. He waited outside my front doorway to see me.

"This donkey will serve us well as a member of our family, Mary," he said shyly, smiling his warm smile. His dark eyes sparkled, and I noted his brown hair falling to his shoulders in soft waves. His arms were muscular from his work.

"Thank you, Joseph. He is a treasure." I looked up at him, smiled, and took the reins, briefly touching his hand.

CHAPTER 3

THE BETROTHAL

There was a sense of excitement in the air, and many eyes followed me as Rachel and I made our way to the well to draw water for the day. Rachel's betrothal had taken place just a month before, so she had much to share with me.

"Reuben was very handsome, and he looked at me so kindly. His hand felt so warm as he laid it on mine at the signing of the agreement. He gave me this bracelet, woven from the grape vines. I love the way the beads sparkle in the sun!" Rachel could not contain her excitement. She stopped for a moment and took hold of my arm.

"You will be so blessed with Joseph, Mary. I'm sure he is the right one for you."

"Our families agree we will be a good match. Joseph actually chose me and asked his family to consider me for his wife. It surprised me to learn this. I don't remember a time when he was watching me or knew who I was."

"Well, you see, you really are meant to be! Tell me about all the plans, and of how your preparations are going."

"We just got back from Jerusalem and Temple to attend my cousin's forty days from childbirth. The baby's father offered two doves for sacrifice and we heard the prayers for my cousin and the baby, as well as for my upcoming betrothal. It is so exciting to be in the city, and so different from our little village. There are so many people. We left early in the morning, and it took six days to get there and six days to get back. Family we only see when we make the trip to Temple made room for us. They seemed to all be excited for my upcoming celebration, and many are coming to Nazareth. It's all so overwhelming!"

"Your sandals must be completely worn through after all that walking!" Rachel laughed as she looked at my feet. "You will need a new pair for the celebration!"

"Father let me ride on the donkey for part of the trip, maybe because I was walking too slowly!" I smiled as I remembered his kind encouragement. "The donkey walks as slow as me." After waiting patiently in line, I lowered my jug into the well.

Rachel shared her upcoming plans, breathless with excitement. "My family is beginning to prepare for the marriage ceremony already, and it is almost a year away. I am guessing it will take place before the vineyards bloom or just when they begin. That is a long time from now. In the meantime, I have so much learn to prepare for being a wife.

My father is making plans for my dowry." I smiled thinking of my own Father putting together plans for a fair dowry.

My ears perked up to the conversations around me, discussing the Roman soldiers in Sepphoris, a large city nearby. Joseph and his father worked on the buildings in Sepphoris, home to a battalion of Roman soldiers. Fear rose in the women's voices, imagining some of these soldiers coming to Nazareth, where women were vulnerable and Jewish traditions not respected by the Romans. The women talked of the unrest in Sepphoris, the capital of Galilee, as many Jews were resistant to the Roman rule. I could feel their fear, and it made me a bit uneasy.

"Are you listening to these conversations?" I asked Rachel. "It's kind of frightening."

"Yes, and I can tell you I am staying close to Nazareth." Rachel lifted her jug of water onto her narrow shoulder, as I did the same with mine. "Do you think we are in any danger here?"

"Rachel, we must always be vigilant, but we also need to be in prayer for our safety, and God will watch over us." I laced my free arm through hers. "We will be safe." She managed an uneasy smile, and we walked on to the street where we separated.

"See you soon." As she walked away, a chill ran through me, and I offered a prayer for my friend.

I walked into the alleyway between the houses, and again passed the neighboring donkey. My own donkey stood by a pole near the house. I set my water jug down and stroked his head. "Hello, my new friend. You and I will do great things together, just you wait and see." I picked up the jug and entered the house, greeted by a scene of chaos, people shouting orders to each other and Mother on a mat on the floor.

"What is going on?" I asked my cousin, as she met me at the door.

"Your mother tripped on a mat and fell. We think she bumped her head, and she seems to have hurt her hand as well."

I set down the jug and rushed to my mother's side. Father had laid a cold cloth on her forehead and was examining her hand. Two of her fingers had already begun to swell. My aunt brought some bindings and began wrapping her hand, applying a strong ointment to control the swelling. "Anne, you may not be able to do any weaving for a while, so you will have to leave that to Mary. It's time she perfects the skill," she said to Mother.

Thus began the tedious work of weaving. My first attempt looked about a foot wider at the bottom than at the top, since my weave loosened with later pulls. However, the second one came out much better. There were to be two long sections for my dress with a little fringe on the bottom. Two more lengths of weave were for the tunic to wear over the dress. The two dress sections fastened at the shoulder. A belt

I wove and embroidered tied around my waist. Although Mother was not able to operate the loom, she was there to encourage me. We dyed my tunic with a light blue dye made from the indigotin plant, and it looked as beautiful as the sky.

"Mother, I will never be able to accomplish all that you do in a day. God bless you for your patience with me!" Working on the loom as well as the other daily chores left me exhausted in the evening, and I slept like the dead. Every muscle in my body shouted out in protest.

The day of the betrothal finally arrived. Father butchered a small calf for the event in the afternoon and prepared it for cooking over the open fire in the courtyard. Mother, her hand healed, cleaned and prepared vegetables and fruits for the festivities. Families ventured to Nazareth from other cities and stayed in either our home or homes of other relatives.

"Shalom, family! We are so happy you traveled all this way to be a part of Mary's betrothal to Joseph. They are an excellent match, as you will see. Joseph is handsome and an excellent student of the Torah." Mother was very proud and enjoyed repeating this to each family member on arrival.

Although we were crowded, it was fun to visit and catch up on everyone's families and adventures. The men gathered around the fire, while the women all worked inside until it was time to add the vegetables to the fires. Each carried the various dishes to the courtyard and prepared the bounty for all of Nazareth.

I saw Joseph among the men as we entered the courtyard. He caught my eye and smiled, as I looked down and blushed. His father led him to the center of the courtyard, and my father took my arm and walked with me. My donkey followed me. His father placed the betrothal contract on a table.

Joseph spoke these words, "By this ring, you are set apart for me, according to the Law of Moses and Israel." He placed a wooden ring, intricately carved from a tree branch, on my finger. At my father's direction, I placed my hand on the betrothal contract, and Joseph laid his hand on top of mine as a commitment to the agreement. Then Joseph lifted me effortlessly onto the donkey. The whole gathering cheered for us as Joseph walked the donkey and me around the courtyard.

"Mary, when we are together, you will bring great joy into my life," Joseph said as he lifted me from the donkey and set me down easily. "Let us now join in on the feast."

"Thank you, Joseph. You make me very happy." My heart was bursting, so pleased was I to be with Joseph.

We dined on the food and enjoyed the entertainment for the evening. This time the actors presented my favorite story of Noah. Some of them pretended to be animals with horns or made odd gestures as they walked, while Father read the account.

"Today is a new beginning for Mary and Joseph, just as there was a new beginning for Noah and his family and the animals." Father's deep voice resonated in the courtyard. Everyone cheered. Joseph smiled at me with his warm smile, and we eventually parted to return to our homes.

The next day, the relatives who came for the festivities left to return to their cities. The vineyards had produced a bounty of grapes, now compressed into barrels for fermentation. Workers trimmed the vines for the period of rest during the winter months. Women pressed the oil from the olives and used the by-products for food for the animals. We stored green olives in jars for future consumption. The whole town returned to normal activities.

CHAPTER 4

THE SIGNS

Nazareth was nestled below hills and mountains. Climbing to the top of the mountain, one could see for many miles. Yet our community remained solitary because of its hidden geography. One evening late in the fall as we gathered for our supper, Father opened with a prayer. He then began to discuss the events going on around us, yet far away from our little haven in Nazareth.

Father said, "The Romans continue to impose their ways on our people, and continually try to influence our young people with their beliefs and way of life. Our family and our town practice Jewish beliefs and Temple still controls how we live our lives." Father and the other men were angry.

My uncle, Father's brother, added, "The Old Testament prophesies promised relief from all the strife with the coming of a Messiah, a warrior and King who would give us salvation and the opportunity to rule ourselves, Joachim. Our worship is still under the guidance of the High Priest, but we all long to be a powerful nation again as under King David."

I sat silently listening to the men talk of their hopes and fears. I could hear and see the mixed feelings of all my family as we ate our meal of bread and cheese, olives and pomegranates. We were all poor, living from day to day on what we could raise to eat and clothe ourselves. Water was plentiful, and the hills around us yielded food from the seeds we planted. Wild bushes provided berries in their seasons.

After our meal, I collected the bowls and placed them in a small basket. While some of the family visited and talked of hopes for the future, I took the bowls to the creek to wash them. On the way, I offered a prayer, "God help me to be an example to others of faith and protect us."

I felt a presence around me as I walked, as though God had placed me in a huge soap bubble, isolated from the problems of the world.

"Mother, is there anything you need me to do?" I asked as I returned to the house and placed the bowls in a small opening in the wall for storage. By this time, darkness had begun to fall, and the air was much colder outside than inside the house. Several had already retired to their mats for the night.

"No, Mary. All is done for today. Tomorrow we will plant seeds in the fields." She held my face in her gentle hands and kissed my forehead. Her hands were warm but rough from her labors.

I left the house through the front door and climbed the ladder to the roof, where the air was a little warmer, and a light breeze ruffled my clothes as I ascended. I sat tucked into a corner near the short wall surrounding the roof and looked up into the stars. They were particularly bright that night, and the moon shone a colorful spray of light on the rocks of the wall. Shadows of a tall tree danced in the moonlight, offering a feeling of peace. I tucked my shawl around me.

The apparition I remember seemed to rise from the floor of the roof. I shrank back, startled by the appearance and afraid, blinking my eyes and shaking my head to clear the image. Then a deep, yet kind voice from the image said, *"Congratulations, favored Lady. The Lord is with you." (Luke 1:28 TLB)*

I curled tighter into the corner, thinking I was seeing a ghost, and it was about to frighten me off the roof. My mind did not comprehend what kind of being this could be. The spirit spoke again.

"Don't be frightened, Mary. For God has decided to wonderfully bless you. Very soon now, you will become pregnant and have a baby boy, and you are to name him 'Jesus'. He shall be very great, and shall be called the Son of God. And the Lord God shall give him the throne of his ancestor David, and he shall reign over Israel forever. His kingdom shall never end." (Luke 1:30-33 TLB)

I struggled to understand and to speak. *"But how can I have a baby? I am a virgin." (Luke 1:34TLB).* I looked around to see if any person was there with me, or if this was some kind of cruel joke. On the roof, there was only the spirit, an angel perhaps, and me.

"The Holy Spirit shall come upon you, and the power of God shall overshadow you: so the baby born to you will be utterly holy, the Son of God. Furthermore, six months ago your relative Elizabeth––the 'barren one', they called her, became pregnant in her old age. For every promise from God shall surely come true."(Luke 1:35-37 TLB)

Finally understanding the message the angel was announcing, I bowed my head and fell to my knees. *"I am the Lord's servant, and I am willing to do whatever He wants. May everything you said come true." (Luke 1:38 TLB)* The angel disappeared as though drawn straight up into heaven.

I stood and looked around, but there was no sound anywhere, except for sounds from the animal pens and the occasional bark of a dog. I almost convinced myself I was in a dream, but I was very much awake. Whom could I tell? Was it actually true? I remembered prophesy about the coming of the Messiah, and now the angel was telling me I was chosen to bear the child. I lay down on the mat I had carried up to the roof with me. There I felt a warmth, a comfort the extent of which I had never felt before. In the arms of a soft cloud, I fell asleep.

The next morning, I awoke to the usual chores of the day and walked to the fields with the bags of seeds for sowing the crop. The memory of the angel consumed my thoughts. I merely functioned through my duties, even avoiding Rachel.

Every day continued the same until I had almost put the angel's appearance out of my mind. However, three weeks later, when my menstrual cycle should occur, it did not. I checked several times a day for the signs. Days passed without notice from others in the house. One day, I became ill after eating some cheese, drawing the attention of my mother. Mother also noted that I had not used the cloths in the communal tray.

"Mary, are you pregnant?" my mother asked me. She grasped my shoulders and turned me toward her. Barely more than a child, the weight of the world now became reality. The secret was out, and fear and anxiety welled up inside, sending tears to my eyes. I sobbed uncontrollably.

"Mother, I may be, most certainly. Some while ago I was visited by an angel who told me I would become pregnant by the Holy Spirit and bear the Son of God. It is all so overwhelming. I can't blame you if you don't believe me, but I promise I have not been with a man. What can I do? I am so afraid!"

Mother gasped and in a whisper said, "Mary, let's walk outside where we won't be heard. She put her arms around me. "Tell me what has happened."

Through my sobs, I told Mother of the visit in detail, still trying to understand the gravity of my situation.

"Mary, I believe you, but no one else will, and you could be in danger if this is known. What about Joseph? What about your betrothal?" She searched for answers to her own questions, as I obviously had none.

The angel's words came back. "The angel mentioned Elizabeth to me. I need to see her, as she is also blessed with a pregnancy no one could have predicted."

"Definitely, you must go to Elizabeth for your safety. In the morning, we will put you on the donkey and send you to Elizabeth until we figure out what to do here. Your father will talk to Joseph. God only knows what his reaction will be." Mother hugged me. "God has blessed you, my child." She prepared some food for me to take along on the journey, and the next morning I set off for the home of Elizabeth in the highlands of Judea.

Chapter 5

ELIZABETH'S STORY.

Since this was a familiar road, many travelers from Nazareth walked with me. I rode for a while on the donkey, but jumped down about mid-morning to walk beside him. The sun was getting hot and I looked for a shady spot where the donkey and I could rest. I walked with others, all seeming to be in a hurry to get to their destinations. Beside a large rock, shade stretched out to shelter us both. I watched the other travelers for a while. Men passed with donkeys pulling carts loaded with wares to sell. A few women walked together, chattering and laughing. I lay back on a tuft of grass and drifted off to sleep.

When I awoke, the shade had disappeared, meaning it was close to noon. I took some bread and cheese from the things my mother packed for me, and drank water from the flask. There was still about two hours of walking ahead of me to reach the home of relatives. A small creek trickled along the road, and the donkey was able to get a long, slow drink.

"I need to give you a name, my friend. I can't keep calling you 'donkey'. I think you are 'Jasper'. Do you think that name fits you?" I smiled as the donkey looked up at me as though he understood in his simple ways. We set out again along the road, my mind occupied by thoughts of Elizabeth and her pregnancy. My clothes were dusty from the dirt road, and the dust covered my feet as well. My mother told me of relatives along the way, where I could stay on the journey. No one knew of my condition.

On the second day, as I emerged from our cousin's home, a troop of soldiers passed by in the opposite direction of my journey. A chill ran through me, as a few looked down at me from their horses, and I thought of the women's conversations and fears at the well. I ducked back inside the house to wait for them to pass. *Father God, protect me on my journey.* My cousin connected me with others traveling toward Judea. Feeling God's presence, I was confident to continue on my way. The trip took three days and two nights.

My parents told me about the life of Elizabeth and her husband Zechariah, the priest. "Elizabeth is much older than you, Mary, really too old to be having a baby. She and Zechariah are pious and caring people who worship God regularly, but they could not have children. Elizabeth was barren. Then one day when Zechariah was offering prayers and burnt offerings in the Temple, a voice came to him and told him Elizabeth would have a son, and the boy would be great before the Lord. They say it was the angel Gabriel. He told Zechariah they should name this new baby John. Zechariah was very surprised at the news, and expressed his doubt to Gabriel, because he himself was older as well. Gabriel was angered by his questioning, and no longer allowed him to speak, as he didn't have faith in God to perform a miracle, even though all things are possible for God. He will remain mute until John is born."

Since that day, Elizabeth remained in seclusion most of the time, marveling that she was no longer in disgrace because she could not bear children. Now she was six months pregnant.

Soon I could see the village ahead of me on the road. I picked up my pace, anxious to see Elizabeth. She was not able to come to my betrothal because of her condition. Jasper resisted my pace, more content to keep up a slower walk, so I had to keep tension on the rein. Elizabeth's home was on the far side of the town, across the courtyard. Just as I arrived at the doorway and called out her name, Elizabeth rushed to greet me and shouted, *"You are favored by God above all other women, and your child is destined for God's mightiest praise. What an honor this is, that the mother of my Lord should visit me. When you came in and greeted me, the instant I heard your voice, my baby moved in me for joy. You believed that God would do what he said; that is why he has given you this wonderful blessing." (Luke 1:41-45 TLB)*

Her words were such comfort to me. *"Oh, how I praise the Lord. How I rejoice in God my Savior! For he took notice of his lowly servant girl, and now generation after generation forever shall call me blest of God. For he, the mighty Holy One, has done great things to me. His mercy goes on from generation to generation, to all who reverence him. How powerful is his mighty arm! How he scatters the proud and haughty ones! He has torn princes from their thrones and exalted the lowly. He has satisfied the hungry hearts and sent the rich away with empty hands. And how he has helped his servant Israel! He has not forgotten his promise to be merciful. For he promised our fathers——Abraham and his children——to be merciful to them forever." (Luke 1:46-55 TLB)*

It would be hard to describe the comfort Elizabeth brought to me on that visit. She knew of the visit I had from the angel Gabriel even before I arrived. She said the angel Gabriel had spoken to me as well as to Zechariah.

"Mary, God has certainly blessed us with these sons. I thank God every day for this chance to be a mother after all these years. People around me in Judea no longer look at me when I do go out with pity in their eyes for being barren." Elizabeth's eyes shone with love.

"God has granted me this privilege beyond all measure, but there is no telling how the people in Nazareth will react when I return. What about Joseph? He is such a kind and loving man, yet he will have to decide what to do about me. By law he could have me stoned, or he could just divorce me, leaving me with no husband to help raise the child." I looked to Elizabeth for some comfort.

She put her arm around my shoulder to comfort me. "The people of the town may not accept your explanation for the pregnancy, but God will watch over you. After all, you are carrying the Messiah. And as for Joseph, it will all work out according to God's plan for this baby."

The visit made me giddy and light-hearted. I held my hand on Elizabeth's expanding belly to feel the baby move, and wondered about my own child's quickening in several more months.

I helped her with chores around the house, preparing food and washing clothes. We tore some lengths of cloth to prepare for swaddling the baby when he arrived. I stuffed some feathers into a soft sack that would serve as a bed. Some pebbles in a hollowed stick made a noise to entertain the baby. Elizabeth had some servants who took care of animals and stoked the fires for cooking. Because she and Zechariah, the priest, were of Temple, her clothes were much finer than mine, her house less crowded. Elizabeth gave me a dress and tunic of fine linen, something my family could not afford. During the time I spent with Elizabeth, I found comfort and encouragement.

Three months after my arrival, I heard from my family in Nazareth that I was to return home. Elizabeth was about to reach her delivery date. Jasper and I started out the next morning on the road, my heart heavy and filled with anxiety, not knowing what to expect on my arrival, and missing Elizabeth's company.

Chapter 6

JOSEPH

My parents were excited to see me on my return. My pregnancy was barely noticeable at this point, as my robes were full, and my sash was adjustable.

Mother spoke first. "Joseph has told us he plans to marry you, despite your pregnancy and the baby that is not his. We should begin planning right away for the marriage ceremony. Joseph's lineage from King David will make the baby a descendant of David through his marriage to you at the baby's birth."

"Do you know why Joseph has agreed to marry me?" I asked, pretty astounded at the announcement. Elizabeth's assurances came to my mind. *All was God's plan.*

"He did not offer an explanation; he just said he wanted to go through with the marriage. Truly a generous and caring man." My mother shook her head in disbelief.

The marriage ceremony was to be small and quiet. Joseph's family and mine would be the only ones in attendance. His family argued against the marriage, but gave in to Joseph's stern determination. My family looked at me suspiciously, still embarrassed by my pregnancy by an unknown source. I felt a deep sadness at their disbelief, but did understand their reluctance to believe I might be carrying the Son of God. *It was hard enough for me to believe even though the angel visited me personally.*

The rite took place in my home with my immediate family in attendance, and all prayed for the success of the marriage. I wore the dress and tunic Elizabeth gave me. The wedding attendees walked us to Joseph's house, where I would now live with his family. I had no real possessions, except for my dowry, two other sets of woolen clothes, and Jasper. Joseph's family welcomed me, though somewhat reluctantly.

Joseph and I took mats and climbed the ladder to the roof, where we could have a little more privacy. Joseph lay down on a mat and motioned for me to lie beside him. He put his arms around me gently. "Welcome to my home, Mary." He kissed my forehead.

"Thank you. Can you now tell me why you did not divorce me when you found out about the pregnancy?" I lay my head on his shoulder, feeling his warmth and strength.

Joseph lay back with his arm under his head in contemplation. "At first, I thought it was wise to break the engagement quietly. I was actually right here on the roof, sort of staring out into the sky. Suddenly there was an angel beside me. The angel said, "*Joseph, son of David, don't hesitate to take Mary as your wife! For the child within her has been conceived by the Holy Spirit. And she will have a Son and you shall name him Jesus (meaning Savior), for he will save his people from their sins. This will fulfill God's message through his prophets—— Listen! The virgin shall conceive a child! She shall give birth to a Son and he shall be called Emmanuel (meaning God with us.)" (Matthew 1:20-23 TLB)*

Joseph paused, but continued. "I fell asleep, but right away the next day I told your parents to get a message to you to come back to Nazareth so that we could be married. We will remain celibate until the birth. Raising this child will be a frightening responsibility, Mary. Only God knows what is before us, so we must be in prayer for the child."

I lay staring at the stars as Joseph fell asleep. The miracle of the baby and Joseph's agreement to marry me were part of the plan. I laid a hand on my abdomen and offered a prayer of gratitude for the blessings God had given me. Feeling a sense of peace, I fell fast asleep.

The sun was just breaking over the hills when I awoke. My ears perked up to the sounds of the village as I struggled to get my bearings on the roof of my new home. Joseph was no longer beside me. I quickly dressed and descended the ladder to the front door of the house, where family was preparing for the day. They acknowledged me as I entered . . . a chilly response at that.

Joseph greeted me with a kiss on the forehead, his hands gently on my shoulders. "I will be leaving for the week to work in Sepphora with my father. Some of the work locally will have to wait until the following weeks."

With Joseph leaving, I felt terribly alone. I took some bread and cheese and drank some milk before picking up a water jug to go to the well. Just as I walked to the front door, my sister Salome greeted me with an embrace. Salome was older and lived with her husband Zebedee in the village of Nazareth.

"Come. I'll walk with you to the well for water this morning. I thought you might need a companion." She linked her arm through mine as we made our way through the narrow alleys of my new neighbors' houses. Before we reached the courtyard and the well, she spoke sternly. "Mary, you can expect people to stare at you, as they have all heard by now of your pregnancy and quick marriage to Joseph after you conceived the child. Walk tall and ignore their looks. God is with you."

Just as Salome had said, other women in the courtyard stopped their conversations to watch us. One woman cut right in front of me when I reached the well to lower my jug, turning her back to me. The others joined in conversations speaking in low voices. I could only assume I was the subject of their discussion. Even my friend Rachel walked away rather than talk to me. By the time Salome and I walked back across the courtyard, I was choking back tears. "My dear Salome, God bless you for walking with me this morning. I could never have expected this to happen, when I am so overjoyed at being chosen to carry this baby for the Lord."

Salome smiled at me. "Joseph has done you a great honor to marry you despite your pregnancy, so you can live on as his wife. Some of this hostility will pass, but you have to understand how hard it is for them to accept your account of the pregnancy. I believe you, sister. God will take care of you through this, and I will always be here to help you." When we arrived at the door to my new home, Salome left me to Joseph's family.

I worked hard that day and in the weeks to follow, trying to do my best to contribute to the needs of the household and earn their trust. Joseph would return in time for the Sabbath, and his presence brought me great joy. He was so kind and gentle, and he shared my excitement for the birth of the baby. As the baby grew inside me, it became more difficult to perform some of the tasks, and Joseph's family began to intervene on my behalf, giving me more time to rest. We all settled into a routine of work and prayer, prayer and work.

CHAPTER 7

FEAR IN REALITY

Salome often accompanied me on my outings from the house, always concerned for my welfare and the safety of the baby. The baby continued to grow inside me, but was not yet very noticeable. The women at the well became more congenial, having put the circumstances of my pregnancy and marriage aside for other conversation. The oppression of Rome and the infringement on our beliefs always brought out strong opinions. The concept of losing our traditions to Roman customs paralyzed us with fear.

I still shared in washing clothes at the river, sometimes going at odd hours of the day to avoid the crowds washing and laying out items to dry on the rocks. On one particular day, gathering up the household clothes in a basket, I walked through the courtyard and down to the river, enjoying some time alone. Jasper helped me carry the basket, as I balanced it on his back. He had become a constant companion. Salome was tending to her work in the fields.

At the river, I tucked the length of my dress into my belt to stay dry. As I lowered some clothing into the water and began to rub with the fragrant lye soap, I thought I heard the cry of a kitten. Looking around I did not see anything, so went back to the washing. The river rippled and churned around me, the scent of nearby reeds filled my nostrils. A second time, the anguished cry made me look up, somewhat startled. I rinsed out the cloth, laid it on a large stone in the sun, and climbed back up the bank of the river. Taking Jasper by his halter, I walked first upriver, then turned and walked back downriver, looking for the source of the sounds.

Suddenly, I saw her. Rachel lay huddled between some rocks, sobbing uncontrollably, her hair and dress disheveled. Leaving Jasper, I hurried to her.

"Rachel, what is it?" I said quietly, so as not to alarm her with my presence.

"Mary, he hurt me!" she sobbed.

"Who hurt you? You must stop crying and tell me what has happened to you." I put my hand on her shoulder, and she pulled away from me.

"The soldier. I tried to run, but he chased me on his horse. I cried out, but no one could hear me. He knocked me down, then . . . . " Again, she burst into tears. I stood and looked around, a stab of fear in my heart. Both of us could be in danger.

Again, I tried to console her, putting my arm around her shoulder. "You must let me take you home, so we can see if you are injured."

"No. I can't go home like this. Mary, please take me to your house. Don't let anyone see me."

Helping her up the bank and reaching Jasper, I boosted her onto his back, now sweaty from the heat. Looking up and down the river once more, I grabbed the basket, leaving the clothes to dry on the rock, and we worked our way around the outside of the houses to my family's home. I did not want to take her to Joseph's family.

She slid down from the donkey and we walked to the front door. My mother ran to us when she saw Rachel. "Mother, we must help Rachel. She has been hurt and needs attention."

We moved Rachel to a mat and brought some warm water from the fire to wash her face. Mother gently brushed her hair, not asking any questions, but talking with reassurance that all would be fine. Finally able to control her sobs, she told us her story.

A Roman soldier had raped her. Bruises from head to toe began to turn purple, and her virginity was no longer intact for her upcoming marriage to Reuben. Certainly, the weight of the world was now on her shoulders. She would have to tell her family and Reuben.

My mother and I prayed with her, then walked with her to her home. In the span of just a few short months, we were no longer girls sharing dreams of the future. My dear friend now faced humility and shame at the hands of this horrible man.

We met with the women of the house, who consoled her as best they could. We all knew that Reuben would likely divorce her from their contract, leaving her alone with no hope of moving on in her life. She might even have to go away on her own to find her way in the world outside the support of our community. She could even be pregnant. My heart was broken for her.

In the days that followed, the men of the house watched for the soldier to return. Women going to the river to launder clothes waited for a man or another woman to walk with them. Reuben did decide to divorce Rachel, as he could not reconcile living a life with a woman who had been with another man. Rachel had only her dowry, no longer going to Reuben, on which to survive. There would be little or no chance of a life for her in Nazareth. Two months later, Rachel disappeared, and I never saw her again. Speculation was that she had gone to Sepphora or another city to find a new life. It made me sad to know she did not confide in me. I prayed blessings for her.

Several weeks after finding Rachel at the river, a group of Roman soldiers rode into Nazareth. They questioned several people.

"We found one of our soldiers beaten to death. Who knows of this travesty?"

The people were all silent, looking to one another and shaking their heads. After several more questions, the soldiers left the same way they came, watching each person for a clue to what happened to the soldier. My father put an arm around my shoulder.

"An eye for an eye, Mary." *Was this God's way?*

Time flew by in those months of fear and uncertainty. Finally, as I was nearing the end of the pregnancy, many of us learned we had to travel to Bethlehem, the city of David. The Romans wanted to count us once again to make sure they were not missing any taxes. Because we obeyed the Roman laws as God had commanded us to do, we prepared for the journey. This would mean time away from work for Joseph, and we would have to stay with relatives along the way.

"Mary, I will go alone to register. You should stay behind. The baby is almost due to be born."

"Joseph, no, I want to be with you. I am strong and the baby is by prophecy to be born in Bethlehem. God will watch over us."

Joseph agreed, and I packed enough provisions for the two of us, along with cloths and blankets I might need should the baby be born while we were there. Jasper carried me on his back, along with our bags. Joined by Salome's family and other relatives we made plans for Bethlehem.

CHAPTER 8

TO BETHLEHEM

"Mary, you really must reconsider making this trip. It is some 80 miles to Bethlehem, and you are very near your baby's birth." Salome pleaded with me to stay behind.

"Only Mother is here, Salome. It would be much better for me to be with you and the others as well as with Joseph for the baby's birth. Besides, the prophecy in Isaiah says the child will be born in the City of David. It is God's will that I travel to Bethlehem, and He will protect me and the unborn child." There was no doubt in my mind we had to continue the journey ahead.

"God bless you, Mary. God has certainly chosen a stubborn woman to carry the Messiah!" Salome hugged me and stepped back to let Joseph help me aboard Jasper. My awkward state made it difficult for me to climb aboard on my own.

"I have sent messages ahead to relatives where we will spend the nights. My estimate is that we will arrive in Bethlehem on the eighth day hence, barring no complications." Joseph shared his calculations with Zebedee, Salome's husband. With all of our rations packed, we started out, turning our feet and the donkey's toward the south.

From Nazareth, we followed a path leading to the Jordan River Valley, where the men in our company decided we would be the safest and have more opportunity to rest in villages along the way. During this time, there was danger about, including pirates and thieves. We had little money among us, as we were all poor travelers, but our provisions were precious to us.

"Joseph, please help me down from the donkey, as I need to walk for a while. Jasper and I need a rest from each other, as I am continually shifting my weight. Even the blanket does not cushion that spiny back. The child is active and his movements are creating unbearable pressure." That was in addition to the fact that I had a need to relieve myself. As soon as Joseph helped me down, I ducked behind a rock, lifted my skirts and released the pressure. I waddled back to Joseph and the donkey and continued walking with him for several miles. In the distance, at the top of a rise, we could see our first destination, a tiny village with accommodations for our band of travelers.

Since I had not done much walking in recent months, a couple of blisters appeared on my feet. Joseph carefully washed them and applied an ointment. "Tomorrow you will ride the donkey," he said as he issued a stern but loving directive. "We will add another blanket."

We enjoyed a warm meal and a good night's rest. The next morning, we gathered our belongings and started out again south along the river.

"Take care, my friends," said the owner of the house where we stayed. "There are bears and lions in the hills along the river. Do you have defenses with you?"

"We have brought along some tools from the fields. God will watch over us. Thank you so much for your hospitality." Joseph assured the man we would be safe, but I could not tell if he really believed that to be true. I had never heard him tell of encounters with any animals outside our own domestic beasts.

"Come, let us be on our way," said Zebedee.

"I will walk beside Mary for a while." Salome took Jasper's reins and began walking back toward the river valley. Joseph stepped back to walk with Zebedee. "I have something to tell you."

"What is it?" Salome was smiling and her face was glowing.

"I am pregnant as well. Just a month now. Zebedee and I are very excited."

I reached for her shoulder. "Oh, Salome, how wonderful for you. Perhaps our children will grow up to be great cousins." That thought would one day be very true of our children.

We continued for several miles, before stopping to rest. There was a chill in the air from clouds forming in the north behind us. We stopped among a grove of trees, and Joseph gathered some wood to make a fire to warm us. We passed provisions of bread and cheese among us, along with a flask of clear water from the well. We talked of our hosts from the previous night. Suddenly, we heard the distinct growl of an animal in the grass beyond the trees.

"What is it, Zebedee?" asked Salome.

"I can't see it clearly. Joseph, cut one of those long branches from the tree. We will wrap it in some cloth and set it on fire as a defense, should it attack."

A lion burst from the grass no sooner than Joseph had cut the branch, Zebedee and Joseph quickly wrapped the end in a cloth and set it on fire. Joseph poked at the animal with the end of the fiery stick, while others raised sticks in the air and shouted. The rest of us huddled together in fear. Letting out a cry, the lion first inched forward, then ducked away from the stick. He finally turned and ran away.

"And don't come back!" yelled Joseph, as though the lion understood him. This made us all laugh in relief as we watched the lion bounce through the grass toward the hills.

Joseph struck Zebedee on the shoulder. "Quick thinking!" The men all smiled in comradery, shaking off the fear they had just faced.

We put out our fire and started back on our journey toward our next station along the pathway.

The lion provided our only diversion for the next six days. My discomfort riding on the donkey continued, as the baby was active. I kept shifting my weight. Joseph was gentle and asked me often if I needed rest. Not wanting to slow down the progress, I stubbornly said all was well with the baby.

Finally, at the end of the seventh day, Joseph pointed to a hill in the distance. "On the other side of that hill is Jerusalem. We will stop there at Temple."

"Is the climb over the hill very steep?" I asked Joseph, trying not to show any concern.

"The climb is a steady grade, so Jasper will not have any trouble carrying you, Mary." He smiled his gentle smile, and pinched my cheek. "There will be good provisions in the city and family with warm accommodations for us. We will be there in a few hours. My uncle is expecting us.

CHAPTER 9

THROUGH JERUSALEM TO BETHLEHEM

The family in Jerusalem was warm and welcoming. Our troop disbursed among several homes, but a communal meal fed all of us in the courtyard. We enjoyed a bounty of fish, as many were fishermen in this family. One of the men played a harp for our entertainment.

"Mary, are you doing well?" Salome asked, as she brought a cup of water.

"Thank you, Salome. The baby is anxious to make his appearance in the world, but there are only a few miles left to Bethlehem." I placed my hand on my large belly, feeling the baby move at my touch.

Salome smiled. "You have been very brave. I'm sure Joseph is concerned for you, as am I. With my pregnancy bread and water is about all I can manage right now."

"That will pass, and you will be strong and determined as you await the baby's birth. Will you stay for a while in Bethlehem after you are registered?"

"We plan to stay until your baby is born. From the look of things, that isn't going to be much longer!" Salome hugged me. "You will need some of us close by when your time comes to deliver."

We walked through the courtyard of the Temple the next day, marveling at the size and grandeur, and all the people nearby. Joseph and Zebedee visited with Pharisees, discussing interpretations of the Scriptures. These more liberal men were at odds with the Sadducees, a more conservative group at the Temple. Since this was not an official holiday, the crowds were much smaller.

Gathering our party together once again, we found the path to the south toward Bethlehem. Joseph had the names of several relatives in that city where we might find lodging for our stay. There were eight of us to house: Salome and Zebedee, Joseph's parents, Joseph's brother Emmaus and his wife Rebecca, and us.

"Mary, my father's cousin Aaron and his wife Mariela have a large home on the east side of the city. We will go there to see if they have enough space to keep all of us together." Joseph walked beside Jasper and me, reassuring me of possible lodging.

"I'm ready to get a good rest. Are you growing weary of the travel?" I asked.

"Yes. My father tells me there will be work here in Bethlehem for all of us to earn our keep. We will stay until after the baby is born, for sure. Zebedee will also do some fishing nearby. It will be a welcome relief from travel."

The arrival at the home of Aaron was not exactly what we had expected. Joseph introduced me as his wife. They had already accepted the shelter of other family members, so could only put up six of us in the spare rooms. The alternative was for Joseph and me, being the youngest, to stay in the lower level of the house where the animals resided near the grain storage. The space was clean, and they would provide fresh bedding, along with blankets. Joseph checked with other families on our list, but they were also full of guests, due to the census.

"Joseph, we have no choice. I can't go on any farther, and the facilities, though humble, are satisfactory. Jasper can even stay right next to us!" I laughed, trying to console my husband in his frustration.

"I was reluctant to bring you along on this trip, Mary. Now I can't even provide you with a decent place to sleep. What if the baby comes here in this storage shelter?"

I smiled at him. "Then the prophecy would be fulfilled."

Joseph nodded. "We will just make the best of it, Mary." He brought in our provisions from Jasper, and then brought Jasper down into the animal shelter room as well. Jasper quickly found a fresh spread of straw on which to lie down. He obviously thought the facilities suited him well. The bricks in the walls kept the area cool. Our small room smelled of grain dust, which covered the floor, the animals, and their excrement. Joseph opened a window across from the door to bring in some airflow. A simple structure of hewn logs included a manger and stood between the animals and us. Aaron had arranged some straw bundles around the room on which to lay our mats for sleeping. Two woven blankets lay beside them.

"Well, this turned out to be a decent spot for you two!" Salome joined us and sat beside me on a bundle of straw. "We could have been out in a tent, based on the number of people in Bethlehem today. Zebedee has already gone to catch some fish for our supper. Aaron says the fishing is good."

"I'm going to take a walk about town to see what is available for work. I understand there is some building in progress on the synagogue, so they might need some workers." Joseph was anxious to earn money to contribute to our shelter. He left us there alone.

Salome hugged me. "You are so fortunate to have Joseph. He is such a gentle man, and he cares deeply for you, Mary. Now you should get some rest. If our calculations are correct, you will be having that baby very soon. You will have Aaron's wife, Mariela, your sister-in-law Rebecca, and me to help you when the time comes."

"Thank you, Salome." Salome squeezed my hand and left me to fall into a restless sleep. All sorts of strange visions came into my mind, waking me as soon as I drifted off.

Heavenly Father, bless me in this time of fear at the delivery of the child you have granted me. Send your angels to watch over me when the pains of delivery appear. The prayer calmed me. Joseph returned and rubbed my back until I fell sound asleep.

The next morning we shared a breakfast of bread and cheese and I walked with Salome to the well in Bethlehem for our water. Salome shared her excitement about her own pregnancy, assuring me she would be close by when I needed her.

"What else would I do with my time waiting here for the census to be completed?" She laughed as she hugged my shoulders. "Besides, your delivery will bring me great joy when I see the face of God in your little one."

I smiled at her enthusiasm, noticing a cramp in my abdomen for the first time.

Chapter 10

THE NATIVITY

August is always a very hot time of year by afternoon. Our small room stayed reasonably cool, as there was a window on each side to let in the gentle breezes. I stood by one of the windows and let the wind blow through my hair, lifting it from the back of my neck to allow the air to cool me. Suddenly, I felt the flow of water on my legs followed by intense cramping.

"Joseph!" I called out. He came running from the upper level.

"What is it?" he asked, rushing to my side and taking my arm.

"It's time. The baby is coming. Please get Salome and Rebecca." My breath came in short gasps. The time for the delivery of the child of God had come.

Joseph turned on his heel and hurried out to find Salome and Rebecca. Salome was the first to appear.

"Mary, Joseph sent me to you. Rebecca is getting warm water and rags. You look so uncomfortable. Take this glass of water to drink and let me help you out of some of those clothes." Salome, like me, was a very take-charge person, and was ready to set everything in motion. "We are ready, little sister. You try to rest between the labor pains."

Each time the pains of labor came, I doubled over. My feelings were so confused. I was happy to be having this first child, but I was angry with God for choosing me. Maybe someone older would be more appropriate for this ordeal! The words of the prophet Micah were on my mind. I prayed a silent prayer for the safety of this child. Salome and Rebecca helped me sit forward and rubbed my back. Rebecca too was in the early stages of pregnancy.

"Mary, take some deep breaths when they come," said Mariela, who had joined us. "It will help you to work through the pain." She smiled and put her hand on my shoulder. "It will all be over soon, and you will be holding your baby."

For the next several hours, we talked between the cramps, and each one of them came closer. Shortly after the dinner hour, Salome announced she could see the baby's head emerging. "I see him! He is about to make his appearance!"

"At the next contraction, Mary, you must push with all your might," said Mariela. "Salome, be ready for him to come out. Be sure to lift his head so he can take that first breath easily."

Following Mariela's instruction, I pushed and screamed as the baby emerged, and lay back on the straw exhausted. I could see Salome and Rebecca fussing over him and wiping him clean. Mariela tied off the cord. His crying echoed among the walls of the small room. Salome laid him on my arm so I could see him. God had sent the perfect child. I looked at his little fingers, counted his toes and looked into his beautiful brown eyes.

"Welcome, Jesus," I whispered. *Can he see me? Does he know I am his mother? Does he already know he is the son of God?* He tilted his head toward me, searching for the sound of my voice.

"Salome, there are swaddling clothes among our provisions. If you will find them for me, I will bundle him myself."

Salome quickly found the clothes I had carefully packed, and I diligently swaddled him, tucking his little arms inside the wrapping until he looked like a miniature mummy.

"You should take him to your breast right away, Mary," said Mariela. "His suckling will bring in your milk."

Mariela helped me position him at my breast so he could grasp the nipple and begin to suck. It was much more painful than I could have imagined, as he voraciously tugged. I winced, and a tear stung my eyes.

"That hurts so much, Mariela!" I exclaimed. Every instinct was to push him away.

"Only at first, Mary. It will become easier, and you will so enjoy these peaceful times with your child."

When the baby fell fast asleep, I rose and walked to the manger, where the women had placed some straw for a soft bed. I laid him there, watching him breathe in his slumber. Joseph came in at Salome's request and stood beside me with his arm around my waist. The sky was bright with stars, their beams streaming through our window. I noted how the light reflected in Joseph's face. There were tears in his eyes. An aura of light shone around Jesus' head.

"Such a miracle, Mary. You must rest while he is sleeping." Joseph helped me to the mat and the fresh straw Salome and Rebecca had arranged. I think I was asleep before all of them left me to rest. I had left my childhood behind to become a wife and mother. This small child would direct my life for many years to come.

PART II
WIFE AND MOTHER

CHAPTER 11

Salome and Zebedee, Joseph's parents, and Emmaus and Rebecca all left us to return to Nazareth on the third day after the birth. All had been registered and counted, and responsibilities at home needed tending.

"Joseph, since everyone else is now moving out, why don't you and Mary and the baby move to our extra room? You are welcome to stay as long as you like." Aaron was a gracious host. Joseph was working at the synagogue, a skilled stonemason constructing the outer walls of a new addition. With his pay, he was able to offer food and money to Aaron and Mariela.

"Thank you so much, Aaron. We have managed well, but appreciate the offer. I will move our things right away." Joseph helped me to the extra room with the baby and brought our clean clothes. Salome and Rebecca had taken our clothing to the creek nearby to wash and dry them before they left.

Joseph also set up arrangements to take our new baby to the synagogue for his circumcision and naming. On the eighth day, our son officially took the name Jesus, as the angel had directed us each in those revelations. Oh, how our Jesus cried at the circumcision, but quickly quieted as I snuggled him to me. At the synagogue, we heard that a group of shepherds came to worship there on the night of Jesus' birth, saying they had seen a brightness in the sky along with the singing of angels. They were certain the Son of God had been born in Bethlehem. The priest tried to assure the shepherds they were mistaken, but they insisted he offer a prayer for them and the child. Joseph and I said nothing, but held this news in our hearts, knowing the shepherds were correct.

As we left the synagogue, Joseph spoke. "Mary, we are reminded of the angels' messages to us about Jesus, and the responsibility we have with him. God grant us strength and peace."

We continued to reside in Bethlehem. The Law required we return to Temple in Jerusalem for my purification ceremony and prayers after forty days. Joseph purchased two doves to take with us for the sacrifice. Since we were very poor, our doves would serve as a worthy sacrifice. The Law stated that if a woman's firstborn is a boy, he was to be dedicated to the Lord.

Our journey was uneventful, and at the Temple, we met a man named Simeon who lived in Jerusalem. Simeon exclaimed God had promised him he would not die without seeing the Messiah. He said the Holy Spirit led him to the

Temple on that same day. He held Jesus in his arms and said, "*Lord, now I can die content! For I have seen him as you promised me I would. I have seen the Savior you have given the world. He is the Light that will shine upon the nations, and he will be the glory of your people Israel!*" *(Luke 2:29-32 TLB)*

Joseph and I were a little stunned at his recognition of Jesus as the Messiah. However, a frightening revelation came from Simeon when he said, "*A sword shall pierce your soul, for this child shall be rejected by many in Israel, and this to their undoing. But he will be the greatest joy of many others. And the deepest thoughts of many hearts shall be revealed.*" *(Luke 2:34-35 TLB)*

I was not sure how to react to this. His statement left me very confused. I could only imagine joy in Jesus' coming, not any rejection, and certainly no pain.

As we stood pondering Simeon's words, we noticed an old woman walking hurriedly toward us. Simeon told us her name was Anna, and she lived at the Temple night and day. As she approached, she began to praise God for sending Jesus, but her song of praise also indicated, as did Simeon, that there would be those who did not believe in him. She left us and went about Jerusalem telling everyone that the Messiah had been born. Joseph and I were in awe that these two people knew immediately that Jesus was the Messiah, this tiny child we held in our arms.

When we had completed the purification, we returned to Bethlehem, both of us very silent on our way back. We each reviewed the events of the day in our minds, very confused as to the predictions of Jesus' work and the suffering he might feel. Where I had only felt joy before at the birth of this baby, I was now feeling some fear and anxiety. Joseph was feeling the same, and overwhelmed with a sense of protection for his adoptive son.

At the time of Jesus' birth, King Herod was the residing ruler in Judea. Astronomers came to Bethlehem from Ur, claiming to have seen a predicted phenomenon in the sky. From this, they determined the King of the Jews had been born. When Herod heard of their quest, he sent them a message. He commanded that when they found the baby they should let Herod know so he could also worship him.

Evidently, these men used their calculations to determine where the Messiah was born in Bethlehem. They rode their animals right up to Aaron's house.

"Joseph, there are three men on camels here, requesting to see Jesus." Aaron was a little apprehensive and uncomfortable at their request. Joseph rose and went with Aaron to greet the visitors. Shortly, he brought them to our room.

"Mary, these men have seen signs in the sky that indicate the birth of Jesus." Joseph stood aside and let the men come in. They were all dressed in fine garments and each carried a special gift. I held Jesus closer to me, not sure what to expect from them. I thought for a moment of the bright stars Joseph and I saw on the night Jesus was born.

The oldest of them spoke. "We have come to offer gifts and to worship the child born according to the prophecies of Micah (Micah 5:1-2 TLB). Please accept these and use them according to your needs and those of the child. King Herod has asked that we tell him where he can see the child, but we do not trust him. Please be careful, and God be with you."

With that, they left as quickly as they had appeared. I learned they returned to their land by another route, so as not to encounter King Herod. We were astonished at the gifts, more riches than either Joseph or I had ever seen. There was gold, frankincense, and myrrh, all predicted in the book of Isaiah. (*Isaiah 60:6 TLB*)

"What does all this mean?" asked Joseph, knowing I did not have an answer to his question. We put the gifts under a blanket in our room and retired for the night. The next morning, Joseph had a profound announcement.

Following the departure of the wise men, "After they were gone, an angel of the Lord appeared to Joseph in a dream. 'Get up and flee to Egypt with the baby and his mother,' the angel said, 'and stay there until I tell you to return, for King Herod is going to try to kill the child.' That same night he left for Egypt with Mary and the baby, and stayed there until King Herod's death. This fulfilled the prophet's prediction, 'I have called my Son from Egypt.'" (Matthew 2:13-15 TLB)

"Mary, we are leaving to go to Egypt. An angel came to me in a dream, telling me that we are in danger from King Herod, and we are to go to Egypt for refuge. I have relatives there, and I will have work in Alexandria as well." Without another word from me, we packed up our belongings, said goodbye to Aaron and Mariela, and started out on the long trip to Egypt with our beautiful son and our beloved Jasper. The angels had guided us this far, so in my heart I knew we had to leave.

CHAPTER 12

EGYPT

I have never felt as vulnerable as when we started out for Egypt. The trip would take many days and the area was so desolate. For this particular journey, God had spoken to Joseph and not to me, so I had to trust Joseph was taking care of our precious son. I was a little offended at not being the one chosen to hear from an angel, but I accepted my role now as a wife, submissive to my husband.

We walked along the travel route to Egypt for a few days, stopping in small villages or shelters along the way to rest. We were very tired by the afternoons, worn out from the walking and the heat of the desert.

"What do we have here?" Two riders came up behind us on horseback. Their garments were torn and dirty, their hair disheveled. "Looks like a little family on their way to somewhere. What do you have of value we can take for ourselves?" The more menacing of the two was taunting Joseph, dismounting and talking directly into Joseph's face.

Joseph stepped back. "Please leave us be. We are a poor family with a small child on our way to Alexandria in Egypt. We have nothing of value." Joseph stood up to them. I covered Jesus' head with my scarf and looked away from them.

"Let them be," said the second man. "Can't you see they are alone and afraid?" He sat forward on his saddle. "You shouldn't be traveling alone," he said, speaking to Joseph.

"You are never going to be a good thief!" said the first man. "Okay, be on your way." He motioned to Joseph. Speaking again he said, "There is a caravan traveling to Egypt just behind us. You should travel with them for protection." The two of them rode ahead, leaving us trembling.

"Joseph, we have the gifts in our saddlebags on Jasper. They might have taken everything." My hands were shaking from the fright of the brief encounter. Tears stung my eyes, already irritated from the blowing sand. The odor of their clothes and animals still permeated the air.

"I know. Now we will wait for the caravan. I might use some of the gifts to buy our passage with them to Egypt. We were lucky this time that the thieves took pity on us, but the next time we might not be so lucky. It will be safer to be in a group of travelers." Before long, the caravan caught up to us. Everyone in the party was dusty and dirty from the travels. The leader accepted a gift of gold pieces from Joseph to join them.

I distinctly remember the odor of those awful caravan camels. However, they carried a good deal of supplies for the sojourners. We came upon water during the next several hours of travel, so Jasper could drink, and we finally passed into Egypt. The caravan led us to a stopping place where we could rest at the end of that night of communal travel.

"I have the name of my father's brother in Alexandria. He is a tradesman and will be able to help me find work to support us there. Are you doing well, Mary?" Joseph held Jesus as he told me of our plans.

"I am well. Jesus has been good, just nursing and sleeping most of the time. God is watching over us. This caravan was definitely sent to protect us." I smiled at Joseph with assurance of my well-being. He handed Jesus back to me and lay down on the mat in our small room.

"We will be in Alexandria in a few more days, Mary, and will be able to start a new life there until it is safe for us to return to Judea and Nazareth." He took my hand in his. "We can finally be a true family."

Putting Jesus on a blanket beside us, I lay down beside Joseph. His warmth was comforting. Following my purification and our flight from Bethlehem, we had no opportunity to be intimate. He took me in his strong arms, and I relaxed into the moment.

Our trek was long and dusty, the wind blowing sand into our faces. I kept Jesus' face covered and wrapped my scarf around my head, covering my nose and mouth. Joseph lifted us onto Jasper's back, and led our donkey by foot, covering his own face as well. For a few more days we traveled first south, then turned to the west. The caravan would take us all the way to Alexandria on the sea. There were many such stations for the caravan to stop, where we could get food and water and wash our faces. It seemed to take us an eternity, and we were weary travelers.

We at last arrived in Alexandria, left the caravan, and found our way to Joseph's Uncle Andrew's home. The city was busy with many travelers and merchants. Andrew and his wife Elana had established themselves in the Jewish sector of the city, and they openly welcomed us.

"Your home is so beautiful, and the view is breathtaking!" I was very excited and shifted Jesus on my hip, glancing through the archway to the backyard of the home.

"Such a lovely child, Mary," said Elana. "May I take him from you?"

"Sure, you may. He is getting very heavy to carry." I smiled as Jesus looked up at Elana. Her long black hair and dark eyes gave her the appearance of an Egyptian goddess. She was dressed in fine clothes with jewelry on her neck and wrists that shone in the sunlight streaming through the open window.

"Let me show you to your room." Elana motioned to a doorway into a small room, where a soft mat lay on the floor. Everything looked clean and fresh. An open window looked out on a yard of carefully tended plants.

The house sat on a hill at the far end of a courtyard, surrounded by trees, and it overlooked a beautiful meadow. I was relieved and elated to see where we would be staying. We would even have some privacy here. There were other children in the house as well. This was to be our home for some time to come. I whispered a prayer of thanks to God for our safe travels and our new home.

"Joseph, I am so happy to be here. It has been a strenuous journey to get here, but I feel welcome. Tomorrow I will see what I can do to be useful in the family and get acquainted with the city." Jesus had fallen fast asleep on the mat prepared for him.

"This will be a special home for us here in Alexandria. I will go out with my uncle tomorrow to seek work to support us. We will have our gifts in reserve. Here in Alexandria I may be able to exchange these for money to help pay for our stay as well. We will be happy here, and Jesus will be safe." He reached over and touched Jesus' cheek. "God will protect our boy."

That evening, I met all the members of the family who lived in the house, including the children. One of the women had a son about the same age as Jesus. She was warm and friendly, and offered to walk with me the next day to become acquainted with the area. Her name was Rafaela and she reminded me of my friend Rachel from Nazareth in many ways.

"Mary, our sons can become great friends, and we will have many good times together," Rafaela said. She wrapped her arms around her son. Her dark eyes sparkled and indicated her sincere offer of friendship. There was a Greek accent in her voice.

I smiled and thanked her. My protective instinct kicked in, as I thought of Jesus playing with another child, where he might be hurt or fall. *How am I going to be a good mother and protector of this holy child?*

As promised, the next day, Rafaela and I walked around the area not far from the house, as she pointed out the water well, the stream for washing clothes down the hill in the meadow, and places in the courtyard where merchants came to sell their wares. Joseph and I needed to add some items to our provisions, so I looked forward to the day the merchants would come, remembering my own mother and her negotiations.

"This is all so exciting for me, Rafaela!" I exclaimed. "But I must do my part for the household. Just let me know what I can do to help."

For the first time in many weeks, I relaxed. I decided to share Jesus' story with Rafaela. "Rafaela, as a woman educated in the Jewish laws, you will remember the prophecy of a Messiah to be born in Bethlehem? Many months ago, an angel came to me to tell me I would be pregnant by the Holy Spirit and bear the child who would be the King of the Jews. Jesus is that child. He was born in Bethlehem, and God has guided us here to keep us safe from Herod, who has vowed to kill him. I know this is a lot to ask, but I beg you to believe me." For some reason, I felt comfortable sharing the story with Rafaela.

"Mary, I hardly know you, but if God has so blessed you, who am I to question that Jesus is the promised child? For now, we will tell no one else until the time is right. Come with me; let us go to the fields to gather food for our meal. I'll show you how to make a sling to carry your baby while we work."

Rafaela took a long piece of cloth and tied the ends behind my neck. Then she placed Jesus in the wide part of the sling so the wrap cradled him comfortably. With him in this sling, my hands were free to help with the household chores. We gathered lentils, beans, and onions in our baskets. The goats yielded fresh milk. When we returned to the house, the aroma of baking bread aroused our appetites.

Joseph returned to the house excited about his new employment. "Mary, I have found work building new houses not far from here. I will start as an apprentice to a contractor, who says he will teach me all I need to know about construction. Alexandria will be a wonderful home for us."

"You make me very proud, my husband," I said, reaching out for his hand. "Look what Rafaela helped me make to carry Jesus as I work. He can even nurse here in his little cocoon." I looked down at my baby with adoring eyes. He was changing quickly, putting on weight, and making little baby noises. God had truly blessed me. "I hope you will not be angry with me, as I have told Rafaela about Jesus. She will keep our secret until we can tell your family."

"No, Mary. God intends for Jesus to be shared with the world."

Chapter 13

ALEXANDRIA

Alexandria was a long way from my home in Nazareth The distance was shorter by sea than by land, but still spanned many miles. The city was very different as well. Being a city with a port on the sea, there was great wealth and opulence, very unlike our own small town. Joseph was able to make enough to pay our share for the household, and I would practice to become a good negotiator at the markets to preserve our money.

In the home of Andrew, servants brought in water from the well and worked in the fields to raise crops. The fields were a long walk from the house, as the city was taking over the nearby land. Rafaela and I took baskets and harvested figs, nuts, and olives from the nearby trees. Many other foods came from the market. Each item had to be immediately prepared. Olives were pressed into oil or preserved.

Rafaela found me early the next morning, her voice filled with excitement. "Mary, the merchants are at the town center. Let's leave the children with Elana and the servants, and make our way to the market."

My heart sank. *Leave my baby with Elana while I am away?* "Rafaela, I would rather take him with me. He is getting heavy for me, but I will manage. I would love to go with you, but don't want to leave him." I swallowed hard, trying to cover my emotions.

"That's okay, if you insist. Here's a basket. Remember you must wear a veil in the city to cover your face." Rafaela just smiled at me, knowing my fears.

Taking a small pouch with money, I put Jesus in his little cocoon, arranged a veil over my face, and picked up the basket as we left the house.

Rafaela led the way, knowing all the streets leading to the market. She had an air of confidence, while I felt vulnerable among so many people. I held Jesus close to me, feeling fiercely protective. As we came closer to the market, the crowds of people grew, so I stayed close behind Rafaela. The idea that she could lose me in this crowd sent a sense of panic through me. I tried to relax and uttered prayers for safety. The air buzzed with so many people and the merchants chattering, all getting louder in their negotiations. Many people spoke Greek, so I couldn't understand much of what they were saying. Some of the merchants in the stands cooked food, and the aroma of spices drew customers. We bumped into other shoppers as we moved through the crowds.

"Come on, Mary, just keep moving!" Rafaela laughed and motioned for me to follow her. We focused on the tables filled with fruits, selecting items we did not grow in our own fields. I had never seen such a bounty of food. The sights made me almost giddy with what I might buy. With reality setting in, I guarded my money closely, selecting only a few needed items. My back grew weary from carrying my child. He wriggled and squirmed, reaching for items in the market. The sweltering heat baked me in the clothes and veil, until I felt nauseous.

"Let's go back to the house," said Rafaela. I think she could see how tired and uncomfortable I was by looking in my eyes. We walked the distance to her home, and I was relieved to put Jesus down for a nap. We went about our work preparing bread and washing various fruits and vegetables for the next meal. I lay down on a mat and fell fast asleep, only planning to sleep for a few moments.

When I awoke, I felt a panic, not seeing Jesus on the mat where I placed him earlier. I jumped up and started calling for him. He was only about eighteen months at the time, but he was walking and could be anywhere. God had entrusted this child to me, and I could not find him. As I ran to the back door, Rafaela heard me.

"Mary, why do you call for him? He is playing with the other children in the yard." Rafaela scolded me for worrying. "You must learn to relax and let him be with the others. God will protect him, and he is very safe here."

I saw Jesus with the other children, laughing and playing, chasing a ball. I prayed to God to forgive my doubting His faithfulness and protection. Joseph and I talked of the incident that night, vowing to be more trusting of God watching over His son. We continued to watch for signs distinguishing Jesus from the other children. By now, all of Joseph's family in Alexandria knew of our story of Jesus and believed it to be true. I wondered about my own family back in Nazareth, who were reluctant to believe.

Our time in Alexandria was restful and fulfilling, but we longed to return to our home in Nazareth. We had been there more than two years. Finally, we received word that King Herod died, and now his son was in charge of the region. It was again safe for us to return to Nazareth. Joseph was able to secure passage for us by sea, followed by our journey across land by way of Joppa and Bethlehem to reach home. By this time, Jesus was just over three years old, and I was expecting another child.

With money Joseph earned from his work in Alexandria and what we had left over from the unusual gifts, he purchased some land and constructed his workshop in Nazareth.

James was born to us, followed another year later by the birth of his sister, Miriam. I spent any free time teaching my children proper Jewish ways and beliefs, along with stories from the scriptures my own mother had taught me. At the age of five, I would turn over Jesus' education to Joseph, who spoke Aramaic and Greek. Having no formal education, I spoke very little Greek.

Another son, Joseph, was born at about the time Jesus was attending classes at the synagogue, learning Hebrew and the Torah. He was also spending time with me learning to weave at the loom. He had such a keen and creative mind and learned quickly. His help in this regard relieved some of my work. I loved watching him with his younger siblings. Simon was Jesus' third brother and Martha his second sister in our family. Jesus was definitely a good student, but at the school, he caused trouble, asking questions about the teachings. (124:2.2 TUB)

I observed Jesus, a happy young man with many friends. When he turned twelve years old, interesting events took place.

CHAPTER 14

JESUS AT TEMPLE

Jude and Amos were born by Jesus' twelfth year. When Passover time arrived, Jesus was ready to go with us to Temple in Jerusalem, having graduated from the synagogue school. Our large family caravan made the trip to attend the celebration. Jesus was happy to listen and learn from the teachers of the Law. He was so engrossed in those meetings he did not realize his family was departing for Nazareth at the end of the celebration.

The caravan of friends and relatives divided into two parts; the women and young children led the procession, and the men followed with some of the older children. In any case, no one was aware Jesus was not with us until a full day into our journey. When Jesus did not appear for the evening meal, Joseph and I began to inquire whether anyone had seen him among all the people.

My mind filled with panic, as I prayed for calm and trust. Jesus was more than likely back in the city of Jerusalem.

Leaving the other children with our families, we returned to Jerusalem. Three days passed before we found him among the teachers at the Temple. The teachers were all amazed at the depth of his understanding of the Law at his young age. They had evidently also been watching over him in our absence, assuming we would return for him.

"Son, why have you done this to us?" was the first sentence out of my mouth. "Your father and I have been frantic, searching for you everywhere." (Luke 2:48 TLB)

"But why did you need to search?" he asked. "Didn't you realize I would be here at the Temple, in my Father's House?" (Luke 2:49 TLB) I did not fully understand what this meant at the time. As I looked back many years later, I then understood what he was saying. However, at the time it was hurtful and seemed disrespectful to Joseph and me. I was very angry with him. There was pain in my heart from this child of God. It made no sense.

We returned to Nazareth, and Jesus was on his best faithful behavior, helping me with the younger children, as he grew taller and wiser in the months and years to come. All our relatives and neighbors loved him.

For the next two years, life continued in a day-to-day routine of work and study for all of the family. I taught the girls and the younger children, and Joseph and Jesus worked together to teach the boys. Joseph left his small shop in Nazareth to his brother, and Jesus and he began working with a builder in Sepphoris. The community began to recognize Jesus' skills in carpentry.

Just after Jesus turned fourteen, we received a messenger from Sepphoris. His news told us Joseph had fallen in a tragic accident. He did not survive. While Jesus stayed with his work and the younger children, James and I made the trip to Sepphoris and brought Joseph's body back to Nazareth to bury him on the edge of town. I bathed him and wrapped his body, anointing him with the remaining myrrh. Many from the village followed in a procession to the cemetery. This sweet, gentle man would no longer be by my side. *What was God thinking, leaving me alone to raise Jesus and Joseph's children?* Joseph would not see Jesus when he grew to be king of the Jews as promised. That evening I climbed the ladder to the roof and kneeling there, offered a prayer to God to help me through my grief and fears.

I had no choice but to turn to Jesus as the head of our household. I was pregnant at the time with baby Ruth. Our plight certainly added burdens to Jesus, who at some point would become the man God foretold. *Had God allowed all these events to keep Jesus from his intended reign?* My heart was heavy in grief, and I struggled to understand. Although a model young man, there was no indication of his path to being king of the Jews.

Salome came by the house often to share her own challenges with raising her sons, and she helped me where she could. She also recognized the role Jesus played in helping to raise his brothers and sisters. Rumor had it Elizabeth was also concerned about her son, John. John displayed some unusual behavior and dress, although he remained faithful to his beliefs. With Zacharias's passing, Elizabeth was also dependent on her son, but John's ministry left her in the care of friends and family, while he displayed erratic behavior. Salome's boys actively assisted Zebedee with the fishing, and the income from the catches was good for them.

The years rolled by as each of the children took more responsibility in the family. With more of the children working, our financial pressure was relieved. Jesus finally acknowledged James as the head of the family, as he spent many hours training him, and acquired more freedom to be independent. By this time, Jesus was in his twenties with no prospect for a wife. There was also no indication of Jesus becoming the promised king of the Jews.

All of the promises of the past before his birth were almost a fantasy to me. *Was it all a dream?* I continue my prayers for him and ask God to give me patience and wisdom. As Jesus's brothers and sisters took wives and husbands, I had a nagging feeling that Jesus was preparing to leave. I would no longer be near him to watch over God's son.

PART III

JESUS

Chapter 15

JESUS BEGINS HIS MINISTRY

As anticipated, Jesus left our home. Communications came from him during these years that he was spending time among many synagogues and the teachers in them. We did not see him again until he stopped by when he was nearly thirty years old. He left again, traveled throughout the Mediterranean world, listening and teaching among all he met along the way. I pondered every word from messengers, waiting and hoping for Jesus to reveal himself as the King of the Jews. Jesus and his followers came to a wedding in Cana, and I was there to greet them.

During the wedding celebration, the host ran short of wine, an embarrassment for the family. I turned to Jesus for help:

Jesus said, *"I can't help you now. It isn't yet my time for miracles." (John 2:4 TLB)*

But I told the servants, *"Do whatever he tells you." (John 2:5 TLB)* I was so anxious for him to reveal himself, even if it was just through performing a miracle.

Six stone water pots were standing there; they were used for Jewish ceremonial purposes and held perhaps twenty to thirty gallons each. Then Jesus told the servants to fill them to the brim with water. When this was done he said, "Dip some out and take it to the master of ceremonies." (John 2:6-8 TLB)

When the master of ceremonies tasted the water that was now wine, not knowing from whence it had come (though, of course, the servants did), he called the bridegroom over. (John 2:9 TLB)

"This is wonderful stuff!" he said. "You're different from most. Usually a host uses the best wine first, and afterwards, when everyone is full and doesn't care, then he brings out the less expensive brands. But you have kept the best for last!" (John 2:10 TLB)

In the short time we had with Jesus after the wedding, my family met the disciples and heard stories of how each of them had come to follow Jesus. In my time with Luke, I shared my story of God's message concerning my pregnancy, and the series of events that followed. Salome and Zebedee's sons, James and John, were among Jesus' followers. Noting this brought back memories of that time so long ago when Salome told me of her pregnancy.

In the fifteenth year of the reign of Emperor Tiberius Caesar, a message came from God to John (son of Zacharias), as he was living out in the deserts. Then John went from place to place on both sides of the Jordan River, preaching that people should be baptized to show that they had turned to God and away from their sins, in order to be forgiven. (Luke 3:1 TLB) Elizabeth died before John found his new calling. His preaching became widely recognized.

When Jesus came to him for baptism, John immediately recognized him as the Messiah. After His baptism, Jesus spent some time alone in the desert himself, praying, and ready to begin his ministry. He was then thirty-one years old. Pilate was now the governor over Judea.

On his last visit to Nazareth, I held Jesus' face in the palms of my hands. "My prayers and blessings go with you on this ministry. Your brothers, sisters, and I will all be thinking of you. We will also be very happy to see you, should you return to us sometime on your travels. God bless you." Jesus and his disciples left us for Capernaum.

My daily routine with daughter Ruth included the gathering of water from the well and working in the fields, planted by my family. James led the other sons to Temple on occasion, and he often preached at the synagogue in Nazareth. The married couples gave birth to babies, and I enjoyed watching them all play and grow together. But James brought back disturbing news from his travels.

"Mother, you should know Jesus is stirring up the politicians and the Jews with His preaching. Why does he do that? He also has quite a following as a result of performing miracles for those who come to him."

"James, you know Jesus is called to a new ministry as the Messiah. His mission is to dispel old rules and laws for the living word of love and forgiveness."

"Mother, he has healed many people and demonstrated he can perform miracles. But his preaching causes quite a stir among the Sanhedrin, and I'm concerned for his welfare and for that of the disciples." James held my shoulders in his hands. "We really need to talk to him. I'll find out where they are, and perhaps we can go to him as a family."

Was this what God intended for Jesus? Should we interfere? My heart felt heavy, fearing for his safety, but still not completely sure he was on track with what God intended. James persevered and found Jesus in Capernaum at the home of Zebedee where he and Salome had moved. Crowds always gathered around him, but my family and I waited to see him. A messenger told Jesus his family was waiting.

He remarked, "Who is my mother? Who are my brothers?" He pointed to his disciples. "Look!" he said, "these are my mother and brothers." Then he added, "Anyone who obeys my Father in heaven is my brother, sister, and mother!" (Mathew 12:49-50 TLB)

My heart sank at those words, and my mind struggled to understand the meaning. *How could God allow Jesus to reject me, his birth mother?* I offered a silent prayer to God for his safety. With heavy hearts, we all returned to Nazareth to our daily lives. Many reports of Jesus's preaching reached us and added to our concern.

Chapter 16

JESUS IN JERUSALEM

With my son James spending more and more time in Jerusalem, where he was preaching in the Temple, he helped me move to the city. This was not really my choice of the ideal place to live, but the children insisted. I said farewell to my home in Nazareth and moved my meager possessions to a small home in Jerusalem.

Each day I walked to Temple to pray for Jesus and the rest of my family. "You are his mother? What is he trying to do?!" Some were angry with Jesus, but some were supportive. "He has done so much for the poor and needy. God bless him in his service." Their comments were very hard for me, so I tried to stay in my home as much as possible to avoid the conflicts on the streets.

"Mother, you must come to the road into Jerusalem. Jesus is coming to Jerusalem and people are greeting him there!" Ruth had come with me to Jerusalem, and heard the news on the streets. "They say he is going to make a triumphant entry into Jerusalem, just as God has said." Ruth never faltered in her belief in Jesus as the Messiah. We soon learned that her faith in him was justified.

And those in the crowd who had seen Jesus call Lazarus back to life were telling all about it. That was the main reason why so many went out to meet him—because they had heard about this mighty miracle. (John 12:17 TLB)

Ruth and I hurried to a place along the road to Temple and waited among the crowds. They shouted, *"The Savior! God bless the King of Israel! Hail to God's Ambassador!"* (*John 12:12b TLB*)

I was so excited. Finally, people would recognize Jesus as the promised king of Israel. My heart pounded in my chest, and Ruth and I hugged each other in triumph. We watched as people put olive branches and garments in his path.

The mood changed dramatically when Jesus reached the Temple. He became very angry when he saw all the merchants on the Temple grounds selling various items, and he drove them out. I had never seen him so angry. He also claimed to the crowd to be the Messiah, but that his time on earth was limited.

Jesus said, "The time of judgment for the world has come—and the time when Satan, the prince of this world, shall be cast out. And when I am lifted up on the cross, I will draw everyone to me." He said this to indicate how he was going to die. (John 12:31-33 TLB)

The words that came from his mouth confused me even further, and Ruth did not fully understand either. When he finished speaking, he left the city. We went back to our home, shaken by what we had seen and heard. Ruth and I prayed together.

Unbeknownst to us, the Sanhedrin held meetings to discuss the fate of Jesus and his followers. They obviously did not recognize him as the Son of God. To them he was a troublemaker who defied the beliefs and laws of the Jews. Just a few days after Jesus's triumphant ride into Jerusalem, they arrested him where he had gone to pray with his disciples.

As the company of armed soldiers and guards, carrying torches and lanterns, approach the garden, Judas stepped well out in front of the band that he might be ready quickly to identify Jesus so that the apprehenders could easily lay hands on him before his associates could rally to his defense. (183:3.1 TUB)

At that very moment, while he was still speaking, Judas, one of the Twelve, arrived with a great crowd armed with swords and clubs, sent by the Jewish leaders. Judas had told them to arrest the man he greeted, for that would be the one they were after. So now Judas came straight to Jesus and said, "Hello, Master!" and embraced him in friendly fashion. (Matt 26:47-49 TLB)

Some of the disciples came to tell me about Jesus' arrest. They told me about the Passover they all shared with him, how he had washed their feet, and the ceremonial wine and bread. He would most likely face a trial the next day. They were afraid for their own lives, as people were looking for them. They hid in the room where Jesus shared the Passover the night before.

The next day, within a few short hours of horrifying abuse, Jesus was condemned to die. My tears fell like the rain, my sobs wracking my body. My emotions grew from anger at all those gathered together. God had forsaken His own Son. Ruth tried to console me, as did Mary Magdalene, none of us able to understand how our Messiah's life could be over. His work was still unfinished. Jesus suffered through the abuse, bleeding from the crown of thorns and the beatings. Weak from his treatment, he struggled to the hill where he would die. People who formerly believed and worshiped him walked away. Most of his disciples could not bear the anguish of his death. All they knew, restricted by their human understanding, was lost in his death.

As we stood below his cross, Jesus appointed his disciple John to watch over me. John put his arm around my shoulders as a sign of his comfort. Crowds gathered to watch the spectacle as hours passed. I searched their faces for some sign of guilt, but saw none. Soldiers taunted him and grew weary of the hours before his death. A blackness came over the sky, and wrapped us in total darkness. We stood in silence, tears flowing unabated, awaiting his last breath. When he finally uttered his final words and died, strange events caused many unbelievers to reconsider whether he might have truly been the Son of God. Friends arranged for his burial in a borrowed grave.

Confusion clouded my mind, as I walked to John's home in Jerusalem that night. John stayed with the others in the

Upper Room. I knew Jesus was the Son of God in my heart. He was to be King of the Jews and our hope to return to the time and rule of David. All of the visions we held for Him were shattered. I struggled to understand and prayed for God's revelation.

CHAPTER 17

NEW LIFE

We had no chance to sleep that night. I lay awake, my eyes swollen from tears as I prayed for a miracle. We moved about listlessly, so unsure of the future without Jesus's guidance. On Sunday, some of the women decided to go to the place where they buried Jesus to offer prayers, and to anoint his body properly. Mary Magdalene and my sister Salome were among the five women. No one could have possibly warned them of what happened next.

As the women approached the tomb, the ground shook, and the stone moved away. The light coming from the tomb was blinding, and the guards fainted. An angel spoke, "Don't be frightened. I know you are looking for Jesus, who was crucified, but he isn't here! For he has come back to life again, just as he said he would. Come in and see where his body was lying." (*Matthew 28:5-6 TLB*)

Then the angel told them to go to the disciples and tell the remaining eleven to go to Galilee where Jesus would meet them.

I traveled with John and the rest of the disciples to Galilee. Jesus had expressed to the disciples many times that he would return, although the very thought was hard for any to imagine. When Jesus appeared among us, we stood back in fear. He spoke in His familiar voice:

"When I was with you before, don't you remember my telling you that everything written about me by Moses and the prophets and in the Psalms must all come true?" Then He opened their minds to understand at last these many Scriptures! And he said, "Yes it was written long ago that the Messiah must suffer and die and rise again from the dead on the third day; and that this message of salvation should be taken from Jerusalem to all the nations: There is forgiveness of sins for all who turn to me. You have seen these prophecies come true." (Luke 24:44-48 TLB)

I studied prophesies as a child and turned to the Torah many times to understand the gift of Jesus to the world. Now, finally with Him standing before us to explain the Scriptures, my mind opened to the real meaning of His role as king of the Jews. He and the disciples would spread the Good News of salvation for the Jews–– not in a way related to David as the King, as we had all imagined, but in a way only God could deliver.

Jesus left us that day to go to His home in heaven. Although the disciples recognized me as the mother of Jesus, the truth became clear. I was merely a vessel through which

God created the human Jesus to walk the earth among other men and women, and to live a perfect life. In all of his travels throughout the Jewish and Gentile lands, he gathered knowledge and understanding of our strengths and weaknesses. I now wanted to do my part to spread the Good News as well.

The gospel of the kingdom, the message of Jesus, had been suddenly changed into the gospel of the Lord Jesus Christ. They now proclaimed the facts of his life, death, and resurrection and preached the hope of his speedy return to this world to finish the work he began. Thus the message of the early believers had to do with preaching about the facts of his coming and with teaching the hope of his second coming, an event which they deemed to be very near at hand. (194.4.5 TUB)

As I visited with people at Temple, back in Jerusalem, it was a struggle for Jews to abandon the structure and rules of law to which they had become accustomed. I completely understood. When you grow up among the rules of Jewish law as I had, the idea of a more liberated style of life based on the Good News of Jesus was almost unrecognizable. I could see that the changes in attitude would come slowly over time, except for those who chose to grasp this Christian way of life immediately.

Joy and peace filled my life. The apostles were scattered as Jesus had instructed them, so I only saw John on a regular basis. James remained in Jerusalem to play a more permanent role in Temple. The Sanhedrin and the Pharisees were more open to his preaching and management following the death and resurrection of Jesus. They started rumors among the authorities to the effect that Jesus's body was stolen from the grave, there was no resurrection, and many believed that to be true. Mostly that resistance was because of the human element and lack of faith in the growing movement. My heart is open to forgiveness in this regard, having been so blind myself to Jesus' purpose on earth.

John took me with him for his preaching in Ephesus, where a small house outside the community became my home. His mother, Salome, my ever-faithful sister, came to visit us there.

In these later years, I spend my days in the garden of John's home, reading messages from my children and grandchildren and from the apostles on their travels. I think of Joseph and how filled with joy he might be with Jesus' message, but also the anguish he would have felt at Jesus' persecution. One day, I will join Jesus in Paradise, worshiping at the feet of the Son of God.

Acknowledgements

I am forever grateful to my sisters at the Hill Country Women of Words for their review and input as this story was constructed. My editor, Jane Goltz, helps me keep my wandering mind focused on structure and punctuation. I thank my daughter Heidi and husband Jerry for their early reading and comments. While Mary plays a different role among the various Christian sectors, this story is meant to fill in the spaces in Biblical history with the emotions felt by a woman dedicated to God, as are many of us who read these words.

References

Although there are few direct quotes in this story, my research into Mary's life took me to many writings, and I am grateful for the variety of perspectives.

http://www.historicjesus.com/glossary/jewsofalexandria.html

National Geographic, "The Story of Mary from the Biblical World to Today" Special Edition 2018

http://www.biblestudy.org/maps/the-journeys-of-mary-and-joseph.html

https://www.pbs.org/wgbh/pages/frontline/shows/religion/portrait/temple.html

http://truthbook.com/jesus/jesus-timeline

https://answersingenesis.org/holidays/christmas/a-matter-of-time/

http://truthbook.com/jesus/jesus-siblings-brothers-sisters

http://www.linsayhardinfreeman.com/salome-the-most-hidden-woman-in-the-gospels/

https://www.gotquestions.org/Salome-in-the-Bible.html

http://biblehelpsinc.org/publication/josephthe-husband-of-Mary-and-foster-father-of-jesus/

https://www.gotquestions.org/Elizabeth-in-the-Bible.html

http://www1.cbn.com/BibleArcheology/archive/2010/12/19/five-things-you-didnt-know-about-nazareth

https://www.gotquestions.org/baptism-of-John.html

https://www.families.com/blog/betrothal-and-wedding-customs-at-the-time-of-christ

http://www.thebiblejourney.org/biblejourney1/3-jesuss-childhood-journeys-b/jesus-grows-up/

https://www.gotquestions.org/Jesus-Mary-woman.html

https://www.gotquestions.org/Jesus-Mary-John.html

https://www.gotquestions.org/Mary-mother-God-theotokos.html

https://www.gotquestions.org/what-happened-to-Mary.html

http://www.biblehistory.com/links.
php?cat=39&sub=403&cat_name=Manners+%
26+Customs&subcat_name=Children

https://www.futurechurch.org/women-in-
church-leadership/women-in-church-leadership/
women-in-palestinian-judaism

http://bcejudaism.weebly.com/jewish-life-in-1st-century-
palestine.html

http://www.truthmagazine.com/archives/volume44/
V4405040008.htm

http://www.womeninthebible.net/
women-bible-old-new-tesstaments/mary-jesus-mother/

http://www.womeninthebible.net/
women-bible-old-new-testaments/mary-jesus-

mother/mary-nazareth-world-lived/

http://www.womeninthebible.net/
bible-people-mary-of-nazareth/

https://www.christianitytoday.com/ct/2018/january-
february/cover-story-lord-of-night.html

https://www.ewtn.com/library/MARY/
LASTHOME.HTM

About the Author

Linda Kay Christensen, a former farm girl from central Illinois, has enjoyed many years as a bank manager, a self-employed accountant and tax preparer (CPA), and an online instructor for Keller Graduate School (DeVry University). She earned her undergrad in Business Management and her Masters in Human Resources from the University of Illinois, Springfield. Linda's history in writing has included everything from business communication, teaching, and journaling to occasional poetry and now to her books. The inspiration for these books comes from a series of five prints by C. Clyde Squires given to her grandmother in 1916 as a wedding gift. The characters in these prints come alive in Linda's series of the "five stages of love".

Linda's writing includes four novels, Annie's Love, Sophie Writes a Love Story, Out of Darkness to Accepted Love, and We Promised: A Story of Abiding Love. I, Mary is the fifth and final book of the series. Article publications are in the Creative Writing Institute's Explain! Anthology published in 2016. Two articles for Purpose Magazine are included in the June and October 2018 publications. Linda is a member of the Writers League of Texas and Women of Words in Fredericksburg, TX.

Printed in the United States
By Bookmasters